SUNBIRD
PENGUIN

Published by Ladybird Books Ltd 2012
A Penguin Company
Penguin Books Ltd, 80 Strand, London, WC2R 0RL, UK
Penguin Group (USA) Inc., 375 Hudson Street, New York 10014, USA
Penguin Books Australia Ltd, Camberwell Road, Camberwell, Victoria 3124, Australia
(A division of Pearson Australia Group Pty Ltd)
Canada, India, New Zealand, South Africa

Written by Cavan Scott
Sunbird is a trademark of Ladybird Books Ltd

www.ladybird.com

ISBN: 978-1-40939-126-5
004 - 10 9 8 7 6 5 4
Printed in China

CONTENTS

WELCOME TO SKYLANDS!

Hugo's ultimate guide to the world between worlds!

Infinite Islands

Skylands is the most magical place in all of creation, a world of boundless wonder and mystery. You won't find it on any map – but, if you know how to use your Portal of Power, you won't need to!

Portal Masters

For centuries Portal Masters have protected Skylands from attack. They alone can use the mysterious Portals of Power to leap from island to island – and even to other dimensions. The last great Portal Master was Eon. He was thought to have been defeated by an evil Portal Master named Kaos, but he survived as a wise old spirit. Today, he trains a new generation of Portal Masters. That's you, by the way.

THE WORLD BETWEEN WORLDS!

From Skylands you can jump to any point in the known universe – and a good few points in the unknown universe for that matter. This is why Skylands must always be defended from dark forces. If agents of evil ever triumphed in Skylands, they would be able to travel anywhere in the cosmos – including Earth!

An infinite number of islands float in an unending sea of bright blue sky and rolling clouds. Some islands are peaceful and calm, while others are savage and wild – but all are springboards to adventure.

Skylanders

The Skylanders are a team of brave heroes from many worlds, who have been brought together by Portal Masters to protect Skylands and defend its Core of Light. Each has their own abilities and powers, linked to a series of ancient elements: Fire, Water, Earth, Air, Life, Magic, Technology, Undead and Cakes. Actually, that last one is my little joke.

The Darkness

There are a lot of scary things in Skylands. Zombies for example. And ghosts. Then there are the dragons, vampires, bog monsters and sheep. But nothing gives me sleepless nights as much as the Darkness. It's the source of all evil. If Kaos had his twisted, malicious way the Darkness would spread all across Skylands and into the cosmos beyond. My goosebumps have goosebumps at the very thought.

The Core of Light

Luckily, the Core of Light holds the Darkness at bay. As long as this titanic totem shines we are safe. Which is why that villain Kaos spends so much time trying to destroy it.

ROVING ROBBIES

Unlucky for some – thirteen Rotting Robbies have broken loose from their graves and are marauding through your annual. Find them and write the page numbers here.

KAOS!

WANTED FOR:
Trying to destroy the Core of Light and spread Darkness across the entire universe. Oh, and also for generally being an all-round baddie.

NOTABLE FEATURES:
- Bald head!
- Tattooed face!
- Short, fat hairy legs!
- Whiney voice!
- Smells like rancid cabbage!*

LIKES:
- Generally being evil
- His disembodied, floating head thing
- Evil juice cartons

DISLIKES:
- Eon
- Skylanders
- Trees

MOST LIKELY TO SAY:
"Foolish Skylander fools! Prepare to meet your doom! Mwahahaha!"

LEAST LIKELY TO SAY:
"Why can't we all be friends?"

KNOWN ACCOMPLICES:
Glumshanks, his faithful and long-suffering butler.

DANGER LEVEL:
High! Don't be misled by his height and general aroma. This pesky pipsqueak is a master magician and powerful Portal Master!

* Actually this isn't fair on rancid cabbage. Kaos smells a lot worse!

WHICH ELEMENT ARE YOU?

THE CORE OF LIGHT WAS CREATED FROM EIGHT ELEMENTS. THE SAME ELEMENTS GIVE SKYLANDERS THEIR POWERS TODAY. ANSWER THESE DEEPLY PERSONAL QUESTIONS TO DISCOVER WHICH ELEMENT YOU'RE MOST LIKE!

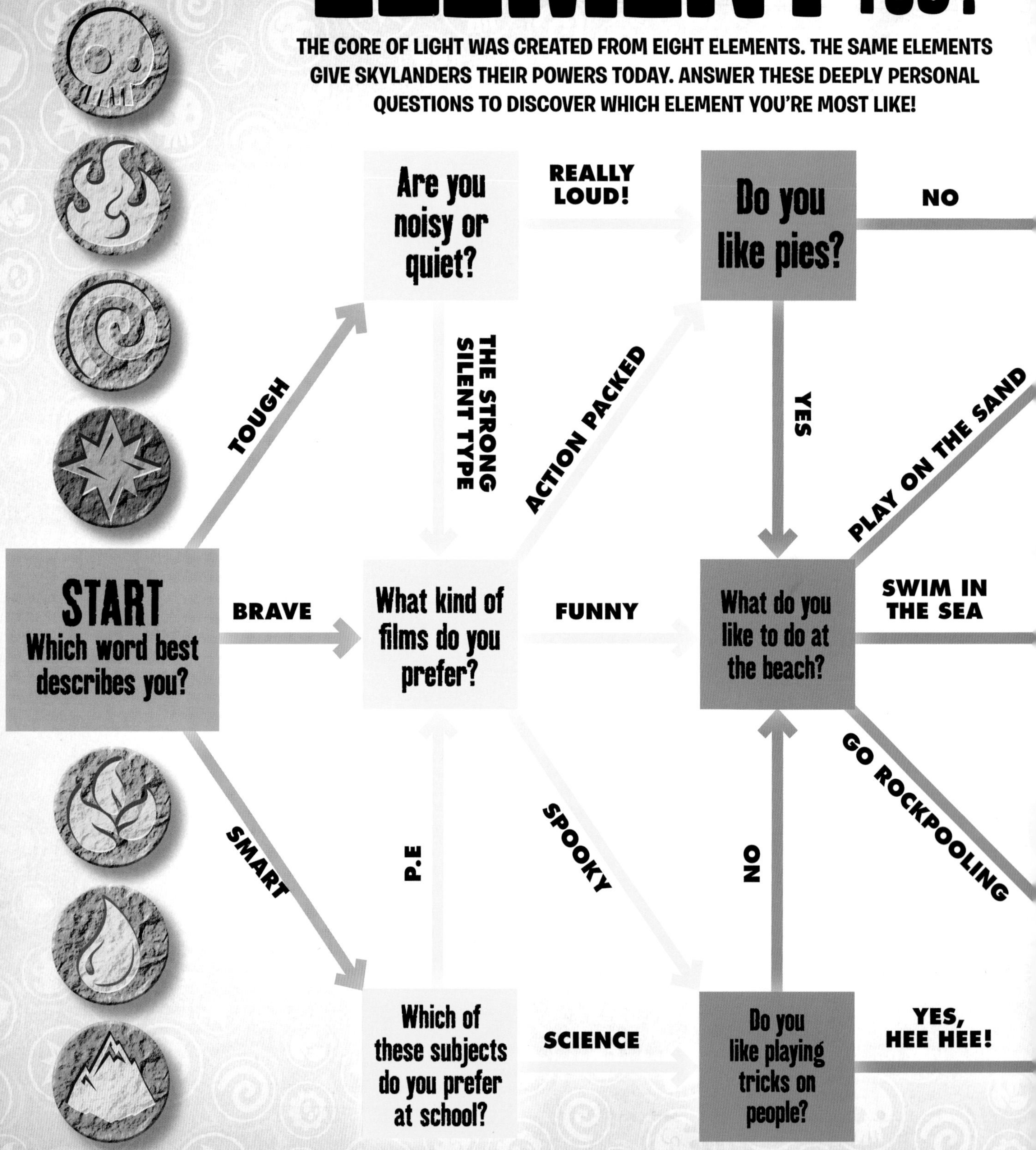

START
Which word best describes you?

TOUGH

Are you noisy or quiet?

REALLY LOUD!

Do you like pies?

NO

THE STRONG SILENT TYPE

ACTION PACKED

YES

PLAY ON THE SAND

BRAVE

What kind of films do you prefer?

FUNNY

What do you like to do at the beach?

SWIM IN THE SEA

SMART

P.E

SPOOKY

ON

GO ROCKPOOLING

Which of these subjects do you prefer at school?

SCIENCE

Do you like playing tricks on people?

YES, HEE HEE!

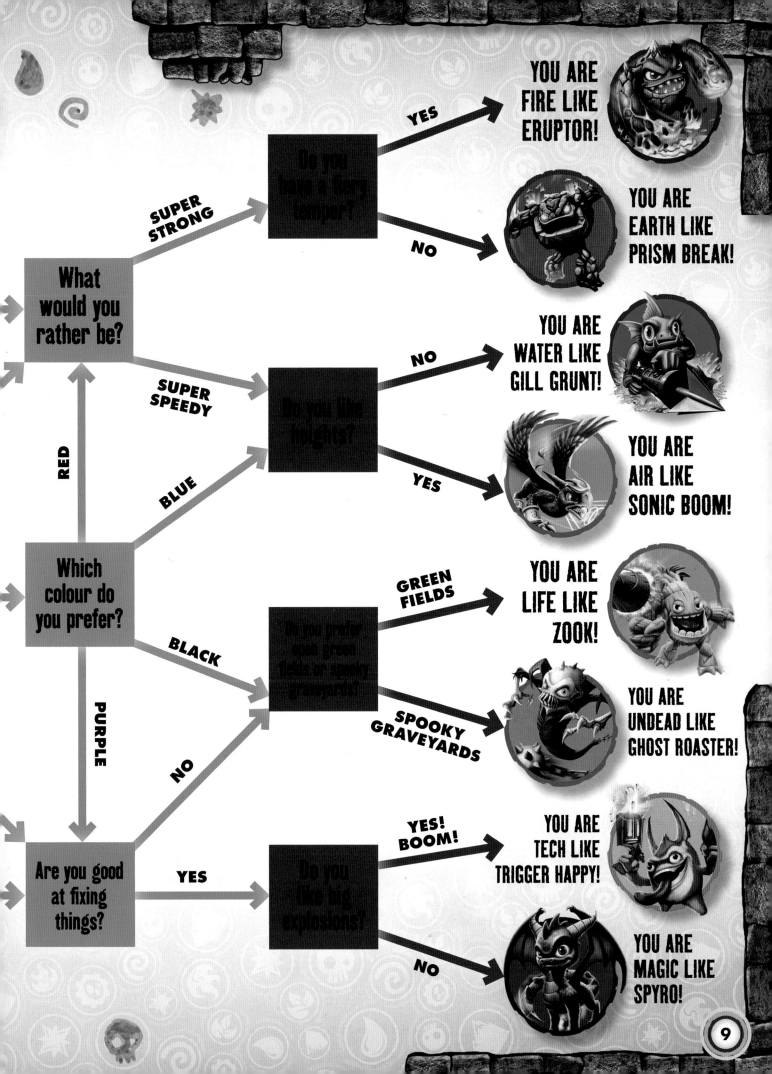

What would you rather be?

- SUPER STRONG →
- SUPER SPEEDY →

Which colour do you prefer?

- RED
- BLUE
- PURPLE
- BLACK

Are you good at fixing things?

- NO
- YES →

Do you have a fiery temper?
- YES → YOU ARE FIRE LIKE ERUPTOR!
- NO → YOU ARE EARTH LIKE PRISM BREAK!

Do you like heights?
- NO → YOU ARE WATER LIKE GILL GRUNT!
- YES → YOU ARE AIR LIKE SONIC BOOM!

Do you prefer green fields or spooky graveyards?
- GREEN FIELDS → YOU ARE LIFE LIKE ZOOK!
- SPOOKY GRAVEYARDS → YOU ARE UNDEAD LIKE GHOST ROASTER!

Do you like big explosions?
- YES! BOOM! → YOU ARE TECH LIKE TRIGGER HAPPY!
- NO → YOU ARE MAGIC LIKE SPYRO!

Ice Scream

"**N**OW THIS IS MY KIND OF MISSION,**"** rumbled Eruptor as Eon charged the Portal of Power. "Blazing sun and hot sand. Perfect."

"I prefer a cool forest glen myself," Stealth Elf admitted, slipping two dragonfly daggers into her belt.

"I don't care where we're going," said Spyro, "as long as there's adventure to be had."

A column of light blazed up from the Portal. Eon turned to the Skylanders. "Remember, this is no holiday. We don't know what danger awaits you on Blistering Beach."

Spyro frowned. Blistering Beach was everyone's favourite holiday destination. Folk flocked from all over Skylands to relax on its golden beaches or swim in the crystal clear sea. It was one of the most tranquil places in the universe, but worrying rumours had reached Eon.

Spyro watched as Eruptor and Stealth Elf dived into the Portal and vanished. There was only one way to find out what was wrong.

"Blazing sun and hot sand, eh?" Stealth Elf was saying as Spyro flew out of the portal. Brrr. It was freezing. This wasn't right. Neither was the snow beneath his feet. The entire beach was covered in a carpet of white.

"Skylanders, thank heavens you came."

A shivering Mabu wearing swimming trunks and a long woolly scarf trudged through the snow towards them. It was so deep that his tiny legs completely disappeared with every step.

"I'm Sandyfuzz," he said, his fur almost blue with the cold,

"and we desperately need your help."

"What's happened?" asked Eruptor, his red-hot breath steaming in the bitter air.

"I thought winter never came to Blistering Beach."

"It didn't," said Sandyfuzz, "until that arrived."

The Mabu pointed at the huge creature that was lying in the middle of the snow-covered dunes.

"What is it?" Stealth Elf gasped. The monster had the body of a stupendous snake and the head of a colossal chicken. She'd never seen anything like it.

Spyro frowned. "An ice basilisk, one of the most ferocious creatures in the universe."

"It doesn't look ferocious to me," Eruptor said. "It's fast asleep."

Sure enough, the basilisk's body was coiled in a heap, its beaked head lolled on one side.

"But it's still causing chaos," Sandyfuzz complained. "It sleeps all the time, but its very presence has caused the temperature to plummet."

"Which explains the snow," Stealth Elf cut in.

"Have you tried just waking it up?" Eruptor asked.

"Of course, but as soon as it opens its eyes, anyone caught by its gaze gets frozen solid." Sandyfuzz pointed at great blocks of ice that were dotted around the beach in front of the basilisk. Spyro looked more closely. Each contained a petrified Mabu!

"There must be a way of getting rid of it," Stealth Elf said.

Spyro nodded. "Only one way. A basilisk can be destroyed by its own reflection. We need a mirror."

"Rubbish," Eruptor roared, bounding into action and racing towards the slumbering monstrosity. "What we need is a little lava lobbing." Almost immediately, blobs of boiling hot magma began bubbling in his hands. "Oi, beaky! Let's turn up the heat."

Eruptor pulled his hands back, ready to let loose a volley of volcanic fire, when the basilisk yawned lazily and opened one sleepy eye. A beam of blue light shot out and hit Eruptor in the chest, instantly encasing him in a block of ice.

The monster roared in fury.

"I've got an idea," yelled Stealth Elf. "Let's give it a lot to look at." She was off and running in a flash.

"What's she doing?" Sandyfuzz stammered.

Spyro smiled, watching his friend at work. "You'll see."

Stealth Elf raced around the beach, zig-zagging here and there. As she changed direction, copies of herself appeared in her wake.

"There are dozens of her!" Sandyfuzz exclaimed. Sure enough, an army of Stealth Elf clones now stood on the frozen beach, all standing perfectly still.

"She can create perfect doubles of herself," Spyro explained. "They're decoys. Her enemies never know which is the real one." More and more Stealth Elves popped into existence. The basilisk reared up, beams of freezing light lancing from its eyes. One by one, the decoys were trapped in ice.

"You see," Spyro cried over his shoulder, racing towards Eruptor's block of ice, "it doesn't know which one to freeze first." Sypro lowered his head and rammed into the back of Eruptor's icy prison. The little dragon shoved with all his might, pushing the block towards the monster. The basilisk peered at the ice block, confused by how it was moving by itself. Its eyes widened as it spotted its own reflection in the slick ice. Then, with a scream, the monster exploded into a flurry of snowflakes.

All around, the snow melted away to reveal warm sand beneath, while the ice prisons shattered and fell away.

"That's more like it," growled Eruptor happily, feeling the warmth of the sun against his craggy skin.

"You're telling me," said Sandyfuzz, shedding his heavy scarf as he ran towards the Skylander. He was brandishing three ice-lollies. "Please accept these as a token of our gratitude."

Eruptor frowned, puffed out his cheeks and melted all three lollies with a blast of super-heated air from his lungs.

"Just cool it, sunshine," he said with a grin. "We've had enough ice for one day."

The End

HERE BE
DRAGONS!
Meet the fire-breathing champions of Skylands!

SPYRO

ORIGIN: Spyro hails from the faraway dragon realms of legend. The Portal Masters of old first noticed him and chronicled his many adventures. Finally, Eon invited this young-at-heart hero to join the Skylanders.

PERSONALITY: Impulsive and headstrong, Spyro struggled at first to work in a team. Now he has developed into the greatest leader Skylands has ever known.

SPECIAL ABILITIES: Spyro can breathe scorching fireballs and you don't want to be at the wrong end of one of his charges. Those horns are harder than diamonds.

DID YOU KNOW? *If you need to know something about any of the worlds of Skylands then ask Spyro. He has an encyclopedic knowledge of all the islands.*

DROBOT

ORIGIN: Drobot was born in the highest reaches of Skylands, but was never a strong flyer. While his dragon brothers competed in aerial contests, he tinkered with technology. While exploring a neighbouring island, Drobot discovered a mine of Arkeyan gadgets and built himself a robotic battle suit.

PERSONALITY: He may be incredibly smart, but Drobot doesn't shy away from a fight. He didn't wait to be invited to become a Skylander. He sought out Eon and offered his services!

SPECIAL ABILITIES: Watch out for Drobot's eyes – they shoot out deadly laser beams! And if they don't get you, his spinning uranium blade-gears will!

DID YOU KNOW? *Drobot relaxes by playing chess – against himself!*

WHIRLWIND

ORIGIN: Descended from both dragons and unicorns, Whirlwind was never accepted by either race. That is until she saw off a troll raiding party who were searching for unicorn tails and dragon scales. The trolls didn't know what hit them!

PERSONALITY: As brave as she is graceful. Whirlwind's moods can be as changeable as the weather, but since becoming a Skylander she has tried to keep her temper in check.

SPECIAL ABILITIES: She can fire blasts of rainbow energy from her horn and summon lightning-packed tempest clouds.

DID YOU KNOW? *Whirlwind also uses her rainbow energy to heal her friends during battle.*

ZAP

ORIGIN: Born into the royal family of water dragons, the young prince was washed away in a furious storm. Lost and alone, Zap was raised by a swarm of electric eels.

PERSONALITY: Zap excels at everything he turns his claws to, but has a mischievous streak.

SPECIAL ABILITIES: As a child Zap created a special gold harness to mimic the electrifying power of his adopted parents. He uses it to shock his enemies, even at great distances.

DID YOU KNOW? *Zap has a longstanding feud with dolphins. They regularly get shocked by his electric waves, although Zap insists it is accidental. The dolphins aren't so sure.*

CYNDER

ORIGIN: Before she even hatched, Cynder was stolen by the henchman of the undead Dragon King Malefor. Raised to do his wicked bidding, she spread terror until she was defeated by Spyro. When he showed her mercy, Cynder realised that there were better ways to live.

PERSONALITY: Cynder still struggles with her dark past and can occasionally be menacing. But she's learning . . . slowly.

SPECIAL ABILITIES: Her spectral lightning is terrifying to behold – but not as terrifying as her ability to summon ghosts.

DID YOU KNOW? *Malefor was eventually banished by Undead sorceress Hex.*

CAMO

ORIGIN: Born in the roots of the Tree of Life, Camo is half-dragon, half-plant. Pure life force surges through his scales, meaning that he can force plants to grow at alarming rates.

PERSONALITY: A real prankster. One of Camo's favourite tricks is to create fruit and veg that explode in your shocked face!

SPECIAL ABILITIES: Camo is hot stuff. He can breathe out concentrated life force in the form of small suns.

DID YOU KNOW? *When he's not protecting Skylands, Camo tends Eon's vegetable patch.*

SUNBURN

ORIGIN: Found in the heart of a raging volcano, Sunburn is a rare dragon-phoenix hybrid. He soon became the target for countless bounty hunters and dark wizards, until he fell under the protection of Eon.

PERSONALITY: Like all dragons, Sunburn is quite the prankster but hates evil with a passion.

SPECIAL ABILITIES: Sunburn is unique among the Skylanders as he can teleport from one location to another in a sudden burst of flames.

DID YOU KNOW? *Sunburn's feathers are so hot you can fry a troll egg on them!*

COULD YOU BE A
SKYLANDER?

HAVE YOU GOT WHAT IT TAKES TO BE A SKYLANDS CHAMPION? OR, LIKE HUGO, WOULD YOU BE BETTER OFF LEAVING THE HEROICS TO OTHERS? FIND OUT BY TAKING OUR TEST – AND HOPE YOU DON'T TURN OUT TO BE A FOLLOWER OF THE DARKNESS!

1

A TROLL ARMY IS RAMPAGING THROUGH THE LAND, RAISING EVERY VILLAGE TO THE GROUND. DO YOU:

a) Spring into action, take on every troll single-handed and send them running for the hills?

b) Gulp and hide in the bushes. Someone else will come and save the day after all, won't they?

c) Cheer them on! The villagers are doomed – DOOOOOOMED I tell you!

2

WHAT'S YOUR IDEA OF A NICE, RELAXING DAY?

a) Saving the world three times before breakfast. And then doing it again before lunch, tea and supper!

b) Sorting the Ancient Skylands History section of the library into alphabetical order.

c) Enslaving the entire universe! Bwa-ha-ha-haaaaaa!

3

WHICH WORD BEST DESCRIBES PORTAL MASTER EON?

a) Awesome!

b) Magnificent!

c) Eon? That pathetic old loser? He shall bow before the Darkness!

4

WHAT WOULD YOU DO IF YOU HAD A PORTAL OF YOUR OWN?

a) Go on amazing adventures!

b) Pop into town and buy a brand new bookmark.

c) Use it to unleash the Darkness throughout the cosmos!

5 WHEN YOU GROW UP, WHAT WOULD YOU LIKE TO BE?
a) Brave and courageous!
b) Left alone to look at my books.
c) All-powerful!

6 WHAT DO YOU THINK WHEN YOU SEE THE CORE OF LIGHT?
a) I must protect it at all costs!
b) It could do with a polish. Where's my duster?
c) Destroy it! Destroy it! DEEEESTROY IT!

7 WHAT'S YOUR FAVOURITE COLOUR?
a) Red! It's exciting!
b) Beige! It's boring and safe!
c) Colour? COLOUR? There will be no colour when the Darkness rules the land!

8 WHAT DO YOU THINK OF CYCLOPSES?
a) Horrible, smelly servants of Darkness! Bash 'em into next week!
b) Shouldn't that be Cyclopsi? Hang on, I'll look it up.
c) Loyal, faithful servants of the Darkness! Good on 'em!

9 THE MABU MAYOR NEEDS YOUR HELP. ROCK WALKERS ARE STOMPING ALL OVER THE PLACE. DO YOU:
a) Swoop in and reduce them to rubble?
b) Pass the message on to Gill Grunt or Trigger Happy. It was probably meant for them after all.
c) Give them a helping hand by unleashing the Giant Clod-Hopping Hordes of DOOM!

10 SPYRO IS...
a) Cool!
b) Braver than me.
c) My biggest enemy! Boo! Hiss!

VERDICT!

Mostly As: Yes, you've got what it takes to be a Skylander, or even a Portal Master as great as Eon himself!

Mostly Bs: You are a person after Hugo's heart. You just don't see the point of putting yourself in danger's way.

Mostly Cs: Oh no! You're a follower of Darkness! In fact, are you sure that you're not Kaos in disguise?

HUGO'S SKYLANDS A-Z

A TRUE PORTAL MASTER KNOWS SKYLANDS FROM BACK TO FRONT (AND SIDE TO SIDE AS WELL). LET HUGO IMPART SOME OF HIS CONSIDERABLE KNOWLEDGE ABOUT THE PLACE AND ITS HISTORY. JUST DON'T GET HIM STARTED ON THE SUBJECT OF SHEEP . . .

A IS FOR ANCIENT SCROLLS

According to Professor P. Grungally, the Scrolls of the Ancients are the most important record of Skylands' long history . . . and even longer future. They speak of the many mysterious races who have ruled these islands and of a young purple dragon who will one day defeat the Darkness forever.

B IS FOR BAMBAZOOKERS

The strange (and some would say lazy) inhabitants of the bamboo forests live their entire lives standing in one place. The only exception is the Skylander Zook, whose itchy feet led him to explore Skylands.

C IS FOR CALI

One of Skylands' most daring explorers, Cali has discovered more lost islands than were ever reported missing. She laughs in the face of danger and is never afraid of being captured by her enemies, which is lucky, as it seems to happen quite a lot. These days she's most likely to be found training young Skylanders in Eon's citadel ruins.

D IS FOR THE DROW

Evil elves who have turned away from the light and embraced the Darkness. Despite their allegiance to Kaos, like all elves, the Drow retain a love of nature. So watch out – if they spot you picking a humble daisy they're likely to give you a seriously evil look (and possible wedgie).

E IS FOR ELDER ELEMENTALS

In days of old, the most powerful residents of Skylands were the Elder Elementals. These legendary soothsayers could master both the light and dark arts, but vanished centuries ago. The Ancient Scrolls suggest they might return one day. The question is where . . . and when? OK, that's two questions.

F IS FOR FLYNN

The greatest pilot in all of Skylands, even if Flynn says so himself. Which he does. A lot. In fact, listen to Flynn and you'll learn more about him than you would think possible. How handsome he is, how charming he is, how irresistible to women he is and how modest he is! BOOM!

G IS FOR GIANTS

We know three key pieces of information about the Giants: 1. They were powerful Skylanders who roamed the lands thousands of years ago; 2. They rose up to defeat the evil Ancient Arkeyans, locking them in the Vaults of Endless Slumber; 3. They were giant.

H IS FOR HOB 'N' YARO

If it's not nailed down, this master thief will steal it. In fact, if it is nailed down, he'll probably nick the nails too.

I IS FOR INFINITE CLOUDS

There are a lot of clouds in Skylands, stretching as far as the eye can see and beyond. Professor P. Grungally tells me that a robot by the name of Kal-Cool-A-Tor once tried to count them all. Sadly, he lost count at around 910 billion and had to start again.

J IS FOR JOKERS

Oh yes, herding a load of bleating, untrustworthy sheep into my library is so funny, isn't it? Just wait 'til I find out which Skylander is behind it (in fact, you can help me uncover the culprit on page 56).

K IS FOR KNIGHTMARES

What makes a haunted house even creepier? The fact that most of the suits of armour are in fact possessed by sword-wielding Shadow Knights. Splashing them with water and waiting for them to rust is not a viable defence. Trust me, I've tried.

L IS FOR LEVIATHANS

Help! Is that a shark in the water? You wish! It's a 20-tonne, ferocious leviathan. Its maw is packed with 1672 needle-like teeth. This titanic terror could eat you for breakfast. And dinner, tea and supper for that matter.

M IS FOR MERMAID

Poor old Gill Grunt. The courageous, guppy-eyed Gillman once fell head-over-flippers in love with an enchanting mermaid from the misty cloud lagoons. Their romance was scuppered when crusty pirates kidnapped his beloved. He still searches for her today. Sniff. It's so sad.

N IS FOR NAUTELOID

These barb-billed beasties live on beaches all across Skylands and don't much like visitors. If you venture too near their hides, they'll scuttle out and try to saw off your ankles, which could seriously ruin a nice day at the seaside. Best avoided.

O IS FOR OCCULOUS

A giant, disembodied eye-thing who crowned himself King of the Ghosts. A little-known fact is that Occulous is incredibly short-sighted. Sadly, none of his subjects could afford to make glasses (or perhaps a monocle) big enough to fit him, so the Lord of the Undead kept bumping into things and stubbing his tentacles. No wonder he was always so crabby.

P IS FOR PERSEPHONE

This plucky little fairy runs the power shop in the shadow of Eon's castle ruins. She'll swap treasure for brand new abilities and powers. No one knows why, but any Skylander who upgrades their powers in her store also comes away with wonderfully minty fresh breath.

Q IS FOR QUIZ

Every year Flynn hosts a quiz about himself. He's also won it for as long as I can remember.

R IS FOR RHU-BARB

There's nothing tasty about these scarlet berserkers from another dimension. Undead Spell Punks just love summoning them into our world and letting them loose. Watch out for those razor-sharp knife arms. They could do someone a real mischief.

S IS FOR SPELL PUNKS

Nasty pieces of work, Spell Punks. These free-floating freaks are masters of magic and mesmerism, but never use their great powers for good. Instead, they've thrown their lot in with the Darkness. No-one knows what they look like beneath those giant cowls, but many suspect that their heads are as pointed as their hats.

T IS FOR TREES

Kaos, that diminutive Darkness-obsessed dum-dum, suffers from an irrational fear that the trees are plotting against him. This is clearly ridiculous. On the whole, trees are peaceful and loving types. Except for the ones that are not, of course. It's best to keep an eye out for them!

U IS FOR UNDEAD

Once the undead dragged themselves from their graves to feast on the flesh of the living. Then an enterprising baker by the name of Batterson introduced them to the delights of pastry. Now, the slavering zombie hordes of Skylands just can't get enough pies. Meat pies. Fish pies. Fruit pies. They're not fussy. Well, they did used to eat brains . . .

V IS FOR VIOLENT STORMS

While huge, devastating tornados are largely to be avoided, smaller ones are very useful for doing the dusting. Or ridding your fields of hideous, malignant sheep!

W IS FOR WINGED SAPPHIRES

The rarest of all gems in Skylands. These flighty, blue jewels are Persephone's favourite so she's likely to give you a hefty discount if you manage to catch one for her.

X IS FOR XYLOPHONE

It is commonly believed that rampaging Cyclops Mammoths will be put to sleep if they hear Crystal Eye Castle's national anthem played on a xylophone. Unfortunately, the spell only seems to work if the piece of music is played in its entirety. As the anthem is forty-seven minutes and twenty-three seconds long, no-one has achieved this feat without being sent fleeing. Pity.

Y IS FOR YUCK

The word usually used to describe Wrecking Ball's foul burp attack. The rumour that an entrepreneurial molekin has bottled the stink as a particularly pungent perfume for She-Cyclopses is completely unfounded . . . I hope.

Z IS FOR ZEPPELIN

Most inhabitants of Skylands travel from island to island in hot-air balloons, but all dread the sight of a Drow Zeppelin swinging into view. Not only are they bristling with weapons, the Drow never look where they're dropping anchor. Look out below!

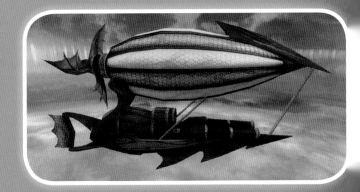

ESCAPE FROM DOOM!

OH NO! KAOS HAS TRAPPED YOU IN HIS DEADLY DUNGEONS OF EVEN DEADLIER DOOM. PLAY THIS GAME WITH YOUR FRIENDS TO SEE WHO CAN ESCAPE HIS EVIL CLUTCHES!

38 MENACED BY A RHU-BARB – GO BACK 3 SPACES

34 A WINDBAG DJINNI BLOWS YOU ON 3 PLACES!

35

36 YOU DEFEAT A SHADOW KNIGHT – GO ON 4 SPACES!

37

33

14 OUCH! A FLAME IMP SCORCHES YOUR BOTTOM! BACK 1 SPACE!

12 A LOCKED DOOR! THROW 4 TO UNLOCK IT!

13

32 ATTACKED BY A SWARM OF CORN HORNETS – GO BACK 4 SPACES!

11 A SECRET PASSAGE! JUMP TO 30!

1 START

31

30

10

9 RESCUE A BUNCH OF MABU – GO FORWARD 6 SPACES

29 NARROWLY AVOID A CYCLOPS MAMMOTH – GO FORWARD 2 SPACES

8

INSTRUCTIONS
1. Place your playing pieces on the start space (sweets make excellent counters!).
2. Roll the die to see who starts. Whoever rolls the highest number goes first (if it's a tie, then roll again).
3. Take it in turns to roll the die and move forward by the number of spaces shown on the die, following the instructions on the spaces as you go.
4. The first person to reach the final square is the winner!

28

27 CAUGHT IN A FAT BELLY SPIDER'S WEB – MISS A TURN!

26

39 YOU BANISH A FIRE SPELL PUNK – GO ON 2 SPACES!

40

41

42 RUN AWAY FROM ROCK WALKER – BACK 2 SPACES!

43

44 A STONE GOLEM BLOCKS THE WAY – MISS A TURN!

16 TUNNEL BLOCKED BY ROCKSLIDE – MISS A TURN!

17 YOU FIND A PORTAL SHORTCUT! JUMP TO 41!

18

5

45 BEAT CAPTAIN DREADBEARD AT CARDS – FORWARD 2 SPACES!

19 AMBUSHED BY TROLLVERINES – BACK 4 SPACES!

46 AN EARTH SPELL PUNK SENDS YOU BACK 3 SPACES!

3 TROLL GUARDS SPOT YOU! START AGAIN!

4 YOU DEFEAT A GOLIATH DROW – GO FORWARD 2 SPACES!

2

5 A TROLL TANK ROLLS OVER YOUR FOOT – MISS A TURN!

20 CORRIDOR BUNGED UP BY SHEEP! THROW A 4 OR 2 TO SHOO THEM!

47

7 GNASHERS BITE YOUR ANKLES – JUMP BACK 1 SPACE!

6

21

48

22

49 KAOS CAPTURES YOU AND TRANSPORTS YOU BACK TO 2. BOO!

25 DISTRACT UNGRY ZOMBIES WITH A STEAK ND KIDNEY PIE – GO FORWARD 5 SPACES!

24

23 HIDE FROM DROW ARCHER – MISS A TURN!

50 SAFE AT LAST!

SKYLANDER SEARCH

HOW WELL DO YOU KNOW THE SKYLANDERS?
ANSWER THE QUESTIONS AND FIND THE
ANSWERS IN THIS WICKED WORDSEARCH.
CAN YOU ALSO FIND THE AGENT OF KAOS
HIDING ALONGSIDE THEM?

```
E V O Q H P T E V X S R D R Q T Q M F G R D W E X I N A D E
Y M A U N R R R T T R R G E P S O A K N U B A X R V M D O R
W P N M T E D I U T I X X D U T C B K T R T R Z C S S X U V
B G A Q P B N M S L V M B N R E Y H O Y Y U N O H C D G B H
Z Y T H V I P A L M O H X Y S A P R O R F G A I Y I L P L D
E Z V A X S O S X O B C H C B L P U T P D S D C A M O X E D
G R V D M R E H B Z Z R B I B T A T R A C X O W Q K B J T K
N V G A T R P C T V O K E Y I H H H O C L H M J E X E O R I
D N S S G B I U Y Z K O S A I E R E N U S K O O K Z R G O D
H H O E S N E D E R L U K I K L E X B Y M W T P D Y K A U V
O H A H O B T Y W M G L E F P F G Y L P T Y H M P Q O P B G
G N H S Y Q R O R C U G A Z M Z G W U J N R Z S W R C V L J
T L J V K N T U C Y M E S B B F I M F N U M F V T T Q C E M
D G D V E I W D X L Z U F S G T R K M Y R C F H J H K V Y L
O Q X J M F Q K A S Y H F Y Z N T W M J G E H K E I M I A B
R R Q S J Z Z C J U I U H I Z M I G L Y L W H A M S H E L L
X N G V D D O R G N I N T H G I L K O Y L L J Y B G R F A L
F L A M E S L I N G E R E P G S P P C R I I E A G S G L G U
X D O D D Q O S A J O O G S N W Y Z W E G L P R E H S Z W M
S P J K A T V H K L K S Y U Y W M N D R D N I W L R I H W
K H B U Y C O M F H J K S F O I X B W Z J W T Y R Z C S N C
N N K G J K W O K S Y R M L D D B A U K W A O S F J L N G Q
I H U N Q F J A S D E E Y Y R G G N R C K J K L C A G A A G
I S R P N H V P F Z J D K F Q R R O T P U R E C M Q P Z Z I
Z D V Y L Y F D U Q R G E N K J E N N X F V N B G P V M V O
A V J M Q L X L I E J E H H E F U A M E T B A E Z V L F R M
L U O N T X E F O U K F M K R X Y U L F N M N X E X A W F E
E R C S H Q V P A B L A Y G F F Z G Z J W C Y B I H H V X C
E F R D J B A R S D S T Y H O A I B U A K O D N Q G L T N X
O K Y S H Y K O H O Z V T Q P H R K R H E N W J D I R S E D
```

1 Half dragon, half plant, this Skylander was born in the Tree of Life. (4)

_ _ _ _

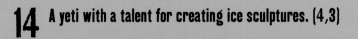

2 Cross an undead warrior and ancient Arkeyan tech and you get . . . (4,4)

_ _ _ _   _ _ _ _

3 A shadowy dragon that turned from evil to good. (6)

_ _ _ _ _ _

4 Which one's which? This wizard can create exploding clones of himself. (6,7)

_ _ _ _ _ _   _ _ _ _ _ _ _

5 An Arkeyan tank that can bulldoze his way through anything. (5,8)

_ _ _ _ _   _ _ _ _ _ _ _ _

6 Hyper-smart with a crazy robotic suit? It must be the dragon known as . . . (6)

_ _ _ _ _ _

7 A lava monster with a fiery temper. (7)

_ _ _ _ _ _ _

8 An Elven archer with flaming arrows. (12)

_ _ _ _ _ _ _ _ _ _ _ _

9 Gobble gobble! A ghoul with an appetite for ghosts. (5,7)

_ _ _ _ _   _ _ _ _ _ _ _

10 This Gillman is one of Spyro's best friends. (4,5)

_ _ _ _   _ _ _ _ _

11 Spooky! It's the undead Elven sorceress. (3)

_ _ _

12 The electrifying hero of Cloud Kingdom. (9,3)

_ _ _ _ _ _ _ _ _   _ _ _

13 Don't try to steal this rock golem's gems. (5,5)

14 A yeti with a talent for creating ice sculptures. (4,3)

_ _ _ _   _ _ _

15 Cover your ears! It's the griffin with the deafening screech. (5,3)

_ _ _ _ _   _ _ _

16 Headstrong and brave, everyone's favourite purple dragon. (5)

_ _ _ _ _

17 Watch out for this elf's deadly dragonfang daggers. (7,3)

_ _ _ _ _ _ _   _ _ _

18 This magical tree loves to drop the hammer. (5,5)

_ _ _ _ _   _ _ _ _ _

19 A wide-eyed gunslinger with a love of gold. (7,5)

_ _ _ _ _ _ _   _ _ _ _ _

20 This is one twisting turtle that will get you in a spin. (7)

_ _ _ _ _ _ _

21 A crustacean who wields a mighty magical mace. (4,5)

_ _ _ _   _ _ _ _ _

22 Descended from both dragons and unicorns. (9)

_ _ _ _ _ _ _ _ _

23 Slurp! A grub with a super-long tongue. (8,4)

_ _ _ _ _ _ _ _   _ _ _ _

24 A water dragon raised by a family of electric eels. (3)

_ _ _

25 Don't get in the way of this bambazooker's barking bamboo bazooka. (4)

_ _ _ _

SECRETS OF THE ARKEYANS

L ONG BEFORE THE SKYLANDERS, A LEGENDARY RACE OF BEINGS RULED SKYLANDS. THEY ARE GONE, BUT THEIR LEGACY LIVES ON. HERE'S EVERYTHING WE KNOW ABOUT THE MYSTERIOUS ARKEYANS.

SECRET BEGINNINGS

The true origins of the Arkeyans are lost in the mists of time – which everyone admits was a bit careless. All we know is that they began experimenting with magic and technology to create incredible new machinery . . . but, as so often happens, they went too far.

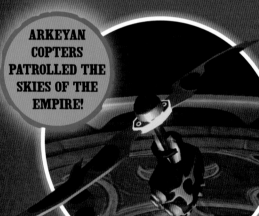

ARKEYAN DEFENDER ROBOTS WERE POWERED BY DARK MAGIC!

ARKEYAN COPTERS PATROLLED THE SKIES OF THE EMPIRE!

THE RISE OF ARKUS!

Soon, their quest for knowledge turned into a quest for power. Led by the Arkeyan King, who wielded an iron fist known as the 'Iron Fist of Arkus', the Arkeyan Empire spread like wildfire.

THE ANCIENT ARKEYAN WEAPON MASTER IS A SOURCE OF GREAT WISDOM – BUT DOESN'T ENJOY TAKING NO FOR AN ANSWER!

MONSTROUS MACHINES

The Arkeyans built terrible weapons of war. It's also said they created a device for cooking the perfect boiled egg!

ROBOTS

The decadent Arkeyan leaders lounged around in the Royal City of Arkus while robots did all the hard stuff, like oppressing the masses, building weapons and doing the housework.

THE FALL OF ARKUS!

Eventually a heroic race of Giants rose up to defeat the Arkeyans. In an epic battle, they managed to lock an elite battalion of Arkeyan robots inside a vault. (Unfortunately, the plans for the perfect egg boiler were locked away with them. The secret of the perfect runny yolk was lost forever.)

ARKEYAN AUTOMATONS HAD SPINNING SPIKES ON THEIR HANDS!

FINISHING THE JOB

With the Arkeyan forces weakened, the Giants went after the King and removed the Iron Fist from his defeated hand – destroying him and deactivating the countless Arkeyan robots spread across Skylands. But the Giants' act of bravery carried a heavy price, and they were swept from Skylands, arriving on Earth – where they have been for 10,000 years.

AN ARKEYAN BLASTER

Arkeyan Blasters can blow anything to smithereens. Batteries not included!

EMERGENCY DRILL

Modern-day Skylander Drill Sergeant was one of the many Arkeyan creations once left to rust underground – but that all changed when he was found by Terrafin!

SHADOW FIGHT!

1

2

3

Before he was a Skylander, Chop Chop was a member of the Arkeyan Elite Guard. Which one of these three shadows perfectly matches the Undead warrior?

Answer on page 62

SKYLANDS SUPERBRAIN!

HOW MUCH HAVE YOU LEARNT ABOUT THE WONDERFUL WORLDS OF SKYLANDS SO FAR? TEST YOUR KNOWLEDGE WITH THIS CRAFTY CROSSWORD. IF YOU GET STUCK, YOU CAN FIND MOST OF THE ANSWERS ELSEWHERE IN THE ANNUAL.

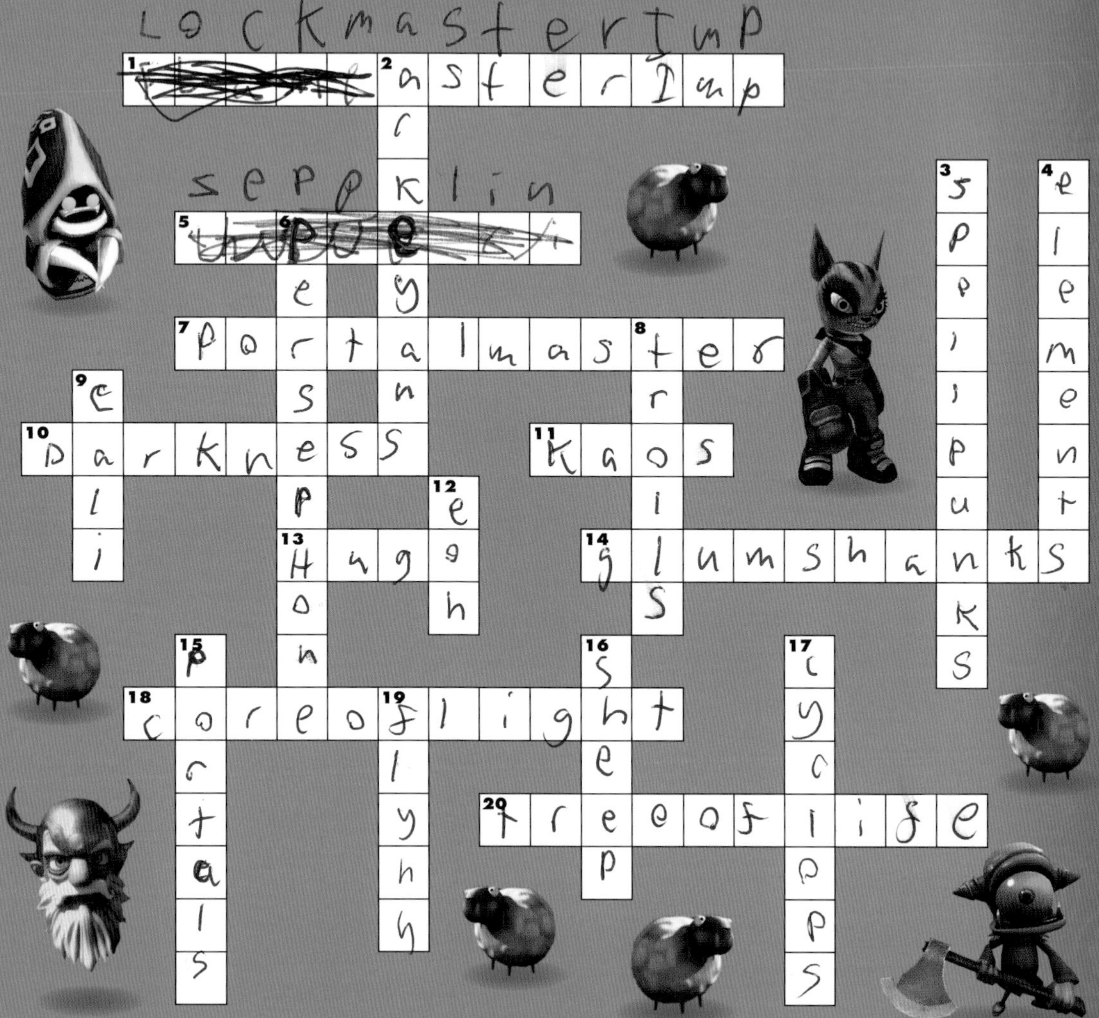

Across

1. A strange little critter that lives within Skylands' locks (10, 3)

5. A huge weapon-filled air ship piloted by Drow and pirates (8)

7. Someone who can use 15 Down to transport themselves across Skylands (6, 6)

10. The ultimate evil power (8)

11. A short, foul-smelling Portal Master with evil in mind (4)

13. Eon's faithful sidekick, who hates the answer to 16 Down (4)

14. Kaos' lanky troll henchman (10)

18. The mystical power source that keeps 10 Across at bay (4, 2, 5)

20. The leafy realm where Camo was born (4, 2, 4)

Down

2. The legendary ancient race that once ruled Skylands (8)

3. Nasty little wizards with big pointy hats (5, 5)

4. Fire, Water, Earth, Air, Life, Undead, Magic and Tech (8)

6. The ethereal, magical fairy who gives Skylanders new powers (10)

8. Stump Smash hates these tiny green ruffians (6)

9. One of Skylands' greatest adventurers. Helps train the Skylanders (4)

12. The greatest Portal Master of them all (3)

15. Magical devices that allow you to jump from place to place (7)

16. Wool-covered critters. Hated by 13 Across (5)

17. One-eyed, pongy monster (7)

19. Pilot, swashbuckler and babe magnet. Boom! (5)

WICKED WILDLIFE

SKYLANDS PUTS THE WILD INTO WILDLIFE! WATCH OUT FOR THESE BEASTS, BUGS AND BOGEYMEN!

CORN HORNET

Notable features: Yellow and black stripes, evil-looking sting.
Habitat: The leafy glades of the Tree of Life.
Fact: Cyclopses love eating corn hornet maggots – especially on toast!
Survival Tip: A sting from one of these buzzing bullies is soothed by applying banana-flavoured gravy on to the affected area.

ROCKET IMP

Notable features: Yellow skin, horns, pointed ears.
Habitat: Troll weapon factories.
Fact: This imp can store explosives in its own body. You don't want to know where!
Survival Tip: Rocket Imps can't see anything coloured camel brown, so paint yourself from head to toe in the colour!

GARGANTULA

Notable features: Six hairy legs, beady red eyes, dagger-like fangs.
Habitat: Anywhere dark and spooky.
Fact: Hugo once found a gargantula in his bath. He didn't dare wash for a year afterwards.
Survival Tip: Be warned – if you defeat a gargantula, swarmer spiders burst out of its body. Urgh!

WINDBAG DJINNI

Notable features: White, fluffy body, ugly face.
Habitat: Mountain tops, cloud kingdoms and anywhere else high up.
Fact: Windbag djinnis smell of stale candyfloss.
Survival Tip: Windbags can blow you for miles. Grab onto something heavy . . . like a passing elephant!

FLAME IMP

Notable features: Wide toothy mouth, long tail on head.
Habitat: Anywhere hot and steamy.
Fact: Flame imps are the most stupid of imps. They sometimes try to eat their own feet, and only stop because they burn the insides of their mouths.
Survival Tip: Get too near and you'll find yourself whipped by that red-hot tail!

STUMP DEMON

Notable features: Terrifying stare, a bite worse than its bark.
Habitat: Haunted forests and creepy crypts.
Fact: Stump demons can live for hundreds of thousands of millions of years (provided they watch their diet).
Survival Tip: The best way of surviving a stump demon attack is to avoid them in the first place.

TRUE OR FALSE

IT'S TIME TO SEE HOW MUCH YOU KNOW ABOUT SKYLANDS AND ITS CHAMPIONS, YOUNG PORTAL MASTER. BELOW ARE TWENTY FASCINATING FACTS ABOUT OUR MAGICAL REALM. THE ONLY CATCH IS, SOME OF THEM AREN'T FACTS AT ALL. SO, WHICH ONES ARE TRUE, AND WHICH ONES ARE NO-GOOD, FILTHY LIES? THE ANSWERS ARE FOUND BELOW.

1 Hugo has an irrational dislike of sheep. In fact, it borders on absolute terror. He thinks they're planning to take over the world. Baaa!
☑ TRUE ☒ FALSE

2 Gillmen are the best singers in all of Skylands.
☒ TRUE ☑ FALSE

3 A race known as the Benevolent Ancients first unleashed the Darkness.
☑ TRUE ☐ FALSE

4 Cyclopses are kind, sweet-smelling creatures.
☐ TRUE ☑ FALSE

5 If you've got enough gold, you can buy the right to be called Portal Master.
☐ TRUE ☑ FALSE

6 When Kaos destroyed the Core of Light, Spyro and the Skylanders were turned into tiny statues.
☑ TRUE ☐ FALSE

7 Portals of Power can also be used to travel through time.
☑ TRUE ☐ FALSE

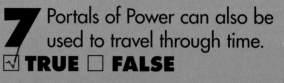

8 The Arkeyans built the Core of Light.
☐ TRUE ☑ FALSE

9 Ghost Roaster's real name is Olav.
☑ TRUE
☐ FALSE

10 Flynn is irresistible to women.
☐ TRUE ☑ FALSE

11 Giants, despite their misleading name, are very, very small.
☐ TRUE ☑ FALSE

12 Trolls have a special day each year when they promise not to blow things up.
☑ TRUE ☐ FALSE

13 Lava creatures like Eruptor remain calm and collected at all times.
☐ TRUE ☑ FALSE

14 Camo once caused a melon to explode all over Master Eon's alarmed face.

☑ **TRUE** ☐ **FALSE**

15 Kaos loves trees.

☐ **TRUE** ☑ **FALSE**

16 Giant turtles have never been seen walking.

☑ **TRUE** ☐ **FALSE**

17 The Undead are scared of pies.

☐ **TRUE** ☑ **FALSE**

18 Flameslinger's magic boots were a gift from an enchanted goblin.

☐ **TRUE** ☑ **FALSE**

19 If Spyro spends too much time in the presence of dark magic he becomes Dark Spyro.

☑ **TRUE** ☐ **FALSE**

20 Lightning Rod considers everyone else in Skylands to be 'girlie' – especially girls.

☑ **TRUE** ☐ **FALSE**

ANSWERS

1. True. Even the sight of a woolly jumper is enough to make him need a lie down.

2. False. Gillmen love to sing, but they sound like warthogs gargling treacle.

3. True. Their foolish experiments with magic first let the Darkness in.

4. False. They are mean, selfish and smell worse than Kaos' old boots.

5. False. It's a talent you are born with. Which means that you are extremely lucky!

6. True. Not only that, but he banished them to Earth too.

7. True – although no one has attempted time travel through a portal for centuries. Or so we believe.

8. False. It was the Benevolent Ancients trying to make amends for releasing it in the first place.

9. True. He was the finest chef in all of Skylands.

10. False. Just don't tell him!

11. False. They. Are. Giant!

12. True. You can tell when it's that day by their unhappy little faces.

13. False. You're kidding, right? They're liable to blow their tops at any moment.

14. True. But Eon didn't mind – and not long later, Camo became a Skylander.

15. False. He maintains a bizarre suspicion that they 'are up to something'.

16. True. The giant turtles of Skylands only ever move as a result of a shove from a passer by.

17. False. They can't get enough of them!

18. False. He was actually given them by a fire spirit he rescued from drowning.

19. True. He uses dark magic to fight evil, but always runs the risk of being consumed by darkness.

20. True. And few are brave enough to argue with him!

Bad Luck Bay

As its name suggests, Lucky Lagoon is one of the luckiest places in Skylands. It's a tropical paradise where nothing bad ever happens. This is why Gill Grunt was surprised to receive an S.O.S from his old friend, Gurglefin. "Come quick," Gurglefin had cried. "Everything's going wrong."

Gurglefin wasn't joking. The usually pristine beach was covered in litter and palm trees were strewn everywhere.

"Oh, thank heavens you've arrived," said Gurglefin, running up to the Skylander. At the last minute, poor old Gurglefin stumbled and fell on his face. Gill helped him up.

"Thank you," murmured Gurglefin, brushing sand from his scales. "I must have tripped on that beetle."

"On a beetle?" Gill said, looking at the insect. It was no bigger than a ladybird. "What are the chances of that happening?"

"Quite high around here," Gurglefin replied, but Gill didn't hear. He was too busy slipping on a banana skin. He landed flat on his back with a painful crunch.

"That was unlucky," Gurglefin commented, returning the favour and helping Gill to his webbed feet, "especially as no banana trees grow in the Lucky Lagoon."

"I don't understand," admitted Gill, finally pushing himself back up to his webbed feet. "Why is this place so unlucky all of a sudden?"

"That's why I called for help," explained Gurglefin. "It's been the same for weeks now. Nothing's going right. First every mirror on the island smashed, then the trees started to fall over for no reason. If that wasn't bad enough a freak storm blew all this rubbish here from the Great Garbage Mountains."

"But they're over 5,000 miles away."

"As I said – unlucky. Oh, and then the island suddenly developed a volcano that erupts every 15 minutes."

The ground began to rumble beneath their feet and a worried Gill looked up at the mountain towering above them. Smoke was already billowing from the crater at its summit.

"We're due another eruption any second now."

"This makes no sense," Gill said, scratching his fin.

"Lucky Lagoon is the luckiest place ever discovered."

"Not any more," Gurglefin carped on. "Not since that cloud appeared in the sky." The downtrodden Gillman pointed up into the air. Sure enough, a massive cloud, shaped like a black cat, stretched across the sun.

"Hmmmmm," mused Gill. "A mysterious cloud, eh? Stand back Gurglefin."

"Why? What are you going to do?"

Gill aimed his water cannon at the ground beneath his feet and pressed the trigger. A column of water shot down, propelling Gill into the air.

"I'm going to pay an old enemy a visit!" he called back, shooting closer and closer towards the cloud. Bracing himself, he rammed into its squelchy side and found himself falling into a hidden lair within.

"Kaos! I knew it!"

Sure enough, the evil Portal Master was sitting in a throne-like chair while Glumshanks worked the complicated-looking scientific equipment that lined the walls.

"This isn't a real cloud," said Gill, fixing Kaos in his sights. "What have you been up to, baldie?"

"Me?" grinned Kaos, thrilled to have an opportunity to boast. "Oh, nothing much. Just being the most evil genius of all time! AGAIN!"

Kaos threw his arms wide.

"This, Skyblunderer, is my crowning glory," he crowed. "My patented luck-sucker-upper™ has drained the Lucky Lagoon of every scrap of good fortune."

"But what's happened to it all?" Gill asked, perplexed.

"It's all been transferred into this rather stylish Good Luck Charm OF DOOM!" Kaos pointed towards the glowing gaudy pendant he was wearing around his neck. "As long as I'm wearing this, I will be the luckiest Portal Master alive. No one will be able to stop me!"

Gill's eyes searched the room, trying to find something to help him defeat the Portal Master. Finally, he just swung his cannon around to face Kaos.

"We'll see about that!" cried Gill.

Whoosh! A spout of water gushed from the cannon, but didn't strike the cackling Portal Master. Instead, it roared over Kaos' shiny head, slamming into the wall behind his throne.

"You missed!" Kaos whooped. "How unlucky."

A smile spread across Gill's face. "I wasn't aiming at you!" Kaos' eyes widened as he spotted the big red button on the wall that Gill had just drenched. Above the button was a dial with two words – 'Good' and 'Bad'. As they watched, the arrow swiveled around to point at 'Bad'.

"No!" screamed Kaos, "You've switched the polarity of the luck-sucker-upper™! It's now gobbling up bad luck!"

The fake cloud lurched as it sucked up all the bad luck that had plagued the island below. Valves burst and sirens wailed, steam pouring out of the machinery. Furious, Kaos lunged at Gill, but tripped over his own feet, tumbling forward. He slammed into the main control console, accidentally flicking a large, important-looking switch.

"Watch out Master," Glumshanks screamed, "That's the self-destruct mechanism!"

Down on the beach, Gurglefin looked up as the cloud suddenly exploded into a ball of flames. Basking in the sudden warmth of the sun, he gasped as three figures tumbled back down to earth. The first to hit the now clean sand was Glumshanks, followed by Kaos himself who crashed to the ground with a groan. Seconds later, Gill landed on top of the defeated pair, grinning from fin to fin.

"Thanks for the nice soft landing boys," he said, winking at Gurglefin. "What a stroke of luck!"

The End

SPOT THE DIFFERENCE

A PORTAL MASTER MUST ALWAYS KEEP THEIR EYES OPEN. MISSING THE SMALLEST DETAIL CAN MAKE ALL THE DIFFERENCE TO A MISSION. TAKE THIS TEST TO SEE HOW OBSERVANT YOU REALLY ARE.

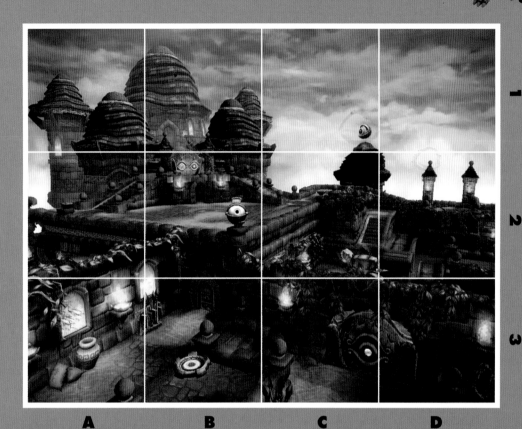

1   2   3

A   B   C   D

HERE'S WHAT TO DO

Look at these two pictures. Think they look the same? Think again! Eon has cast a spell so that there is a difference in every square bar one. Can you work out which square is exactly the same in both pics?

GOOD LUCK!

1   2   3

A   B   C   D

The square that is exactly the same is:

Dear Uncle Hugo

I'M VERY EXCITED. I'VE BEEN ASKED TO WRITE THE AGONY UNCLE COLUMN FOR MY LOCAL NEWSPAPER – THE SKYLANDS COMET. I'LL BE HELPING ALL KINDS OF FOLK WITH THEIR PROBLEMS – JUST DON'T TELL EON!

Dear Uncle Hugo,
I'm suffering from a highly embarrassing condition. Ever since my last birthday I've started to smell really nice. Now my friends laugh and call me names behind my back. What can I do?
Yours worriedly, Anonymous Cyclops

Dear Anonymous Cyclops,
I suggest rolling in a field of fresh cowpats or bathing in a tub of rotting fish. You should start smelling like your old self again in no time.

Dear Uncle Hugo,
This isn't Kaos. But every time I . . . er . . . I mean Kaos tries to take over Skylands, those miserable Skylander fools foil my GENIUS plans . . . I mean, Kaos' genius plans. Don't they realize how annoying this is?
Not Kaos

Dear Kaos,
Have you considered going on a long journey? Like somewhere a long, long, long way away from Skylands and never returning? Go on, give it a go.

Dear Uncle Hugo,
My problem is that I'm just too good-looking. Everywhere I go, gorgeous

women fall at my feet and declare their undying love. The trouble is, there isn't enough of me to go around. BOOM!
Yours humbly, Flynn

Dear Flynn,
Sorry, you're beyond help.

Dear Uncle Hugo,
I've noticed that sometimes people seem to be a little scared of me. I just don't understand why. Can you help?
Lots of love,
Trigger Happy

Dear Trigger Happy
Why are you waving that gun at me? Help!

Dear Uncle Hugo,
My assistant seems to be spending all his time answering questions for his Agony Uncle column. Should I be looking for a new assistant?
Your boss, Eon!

Dear Master Eon,
Eeeeek! I'm very sorry sir. I'll get back to tidying the library right away. Maybe this wasn't such a good idea, after all.

WHEELSPIN!

TAKE A LOOK AT THE SKYLANDERS SURROUNDING THE WHEEL. CAN YOU FIT THEIR NAMES INTO THE SPACES AND WORK OUT WHICH SKYLANDER THERE IS NO SPACE FOR?

Hex

Whirlwind

H

E L y p t o r

ROOK

Gnarltooth

W
H
A
M
S
H
E
L
L

B
a
s
s
h
e
l
l

S
M
N

L
s
a
b
a
b

T
e
r
f
i
n

H
s
e
m
s
p
m
t
s

O
D
b
n
J
W

MY
ANSWER
prison break

Gill Grunt's
Pirate Attack Survival Guide!

Yo ho ho and a bottle of timbers!
Do you know what to do if pirates sail into view?
Gill Grunt is on hand to let you know!

Know the enemy – and how to outwit them!

Captain Dreadbeard

The most villainous pirate ever to sail the 7024 seas is Captain Dreadbeard. His only weakness is his love of card games. His favourites are Trouser Snap, Oscar's Boot and Old Mermaid.
If you beat him at a game, he's honour-bound to let you go.

Evil teeth!

Super-sharp cutlass!

Evil hook!

Evil shoes!

Coarse hair!

Blasteneer

The worst thing about this scurvy wretch is that he constantly smells of wet dog. Oh, and his habit of carrying around a live cannon! Try stuffing sheep into its barrel while he's having his midday nap.

Seadog Pirate

This canine chump thinks of nothing but loot! He spends all his life searching for treasure, only to bury it again. Weird! Your best chance is to quickly fake a treasure map and send him off on a wild goose hunt.

Massive cannon!

Squiddler

These menacing molluscs aren't just interested in treasure. They want to rule the oceans! Luckily, they are terrified of seafood cookbooks. Have one handy at all times, with the recipe for deep-fried squid bookmarked.

Googly eyes!

Mollusc Mortar gun!

Did you know?

Pirates hold an annual sea shanty talent contest – but it always ends in an argument, so no-one has ever actually won.

Anchors ahoy!

Squidface Brute

The real muscle on a pirate ship! So strong he can use the pointy bits on an anchor like a pile-driving pick-axe! Best avoided but, if you can't, move quickly and hope that he gets his anchor stuck in the floor planks!

Cold staring eyes!

Bulging muscles!

Message in a Bottle

Gill has discovered a secret about Captain Dreadbeard. Unscramble the tiles to reveal the message!

FFY	DRE	ED	ET!	ADB	MUM	DS	IM
TO	SWE	FLU	OW	US
EAR	!	H	L	H	CAL

SPEAK LIKE A PIRATE! ARRR!

Pirates are cruel, but they're also a bit dim. If you learn to speak like them, you might be able to fool them into thinking you're a pirate too! Here are a few key phrases:

AHOY!
Hello there!

ALL HANDS ON DECK!
Everyone needs to help!

AVAST!
Stop!

AVAST BEHIND!
My, what a large bottom!

AYE!
Yes!

AYE AYE!
OK, OK. Don't go on about it!

BOOTY!
Treasure!

EVERYTHIN' SHIPSHAPE?
Is everything nice and tidy?

LAND AHOY!
Look! There's some land!

LANDLUBBERS!
Anyone who doesn't like the sea!

SHIVER ME TIMBERS!
What a surprise!

YO HO HO!
How very funny!

ARRR!
I can't think of anything else to say so will make this noise instead!

41

CHOMPIE CHASE

THE TREE OF LIFE HAS BEEN INFESTED BY CHOMPIES. CAN YOU HELP STEALTH ELF THROUGH THE MAZE WITHOUT RUNNING STRAIGHT INTO THE PATH OF A CHOMPIE?

DID YOU KNOW? WHEN A CHOMPIE BITES YOU IT'S NOT BECAUSE IT WANTS TO EAT YOU, IT'S JUST SHOWING HOW MUCH IT CARES. APPARENTLY. AHHH, HOW SWEET!

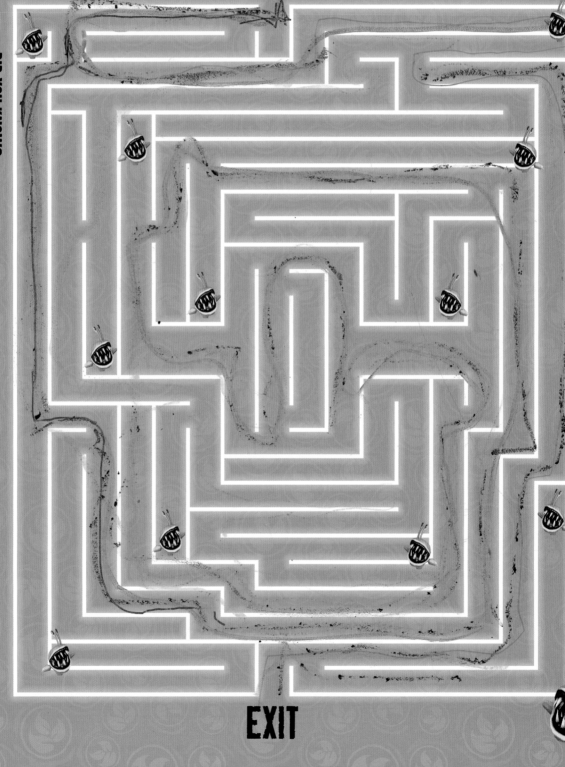

EXIT

HELP WHAM-SHELL DECODE THE SECRET MESSAGE. IT CONTAINS VITAL INFORMATION ABOUT KAOS! WHEN YOU'RE DONE, WHY NOT USE THE CODE TO SEND SECRET MESSAGES TO YOUR FELLOW PORTAL MASTERS?

A	B	C	D	E	F	G	H	I	J	K	L	M
18			14				7	25		13		

N	O	P	Q	R	S	T	U	V	W	X	Y	Z
22	15			24	20	11						1

(handwritten above: KAOS is short, blad)

13 18 15 20 · 25 20 · 20 7 15 24 11 , 19 18 8 14

(handwritten above: lad INS shor)

18 22 14 · 25 22 6 24 17 14 25 19 8 1 · 20 3 17 8 8 1

7 17 · 10 18 22 11 20 · 11 15 · 11 18 13 17 · 15 16 17 24 !

20 13 1 8 18 22 14 20 .

TIPS

EACH OF THE BLANKS IN THE CODE HAS A NUMBER BENEATH IT. FILL IN THE LETTERS THAT CORRESPOND TO THE NUMBER TO CRACK THE CODE. WE'VE STARTED IT FOR YOU.

Need some help cracking codes and cyphers? Here goes:

Look for single letter words. They're probably 'a' or 'i'.

How many times do individual numbers appear in the code? Count 'em. The most frequent is likely to be 'e', the most common letter in the English language.

The most common three-letter words are THE, AND, FOR, WAS and HIS.

SAY WHAT?

KAOS HAS CAST A SPELL THAT HAS MIXED UP THE SKYLANDERS' VOICES. CAN YOU RECONNECT THE CHAMPIONS WITH THEIR OWN BATTLE CRIES?

OBSERVATION DECK

How good is your memory? Study this pirate picture for one minute and then turn the page . . .

QUESTION TIME!

HOW MUCH CAN YOU REMEMBER?
ANSWER THE QUESTIONS BELOW – AND REMEMBER, NO PEEKING!

1 WHICH SKYLANDER DID YOU SEE?

A) ZAP **B)** TERRAFIN **C)** FLAMESLINGER **D)** CHOP CHOP **E)** WARNADO

2 HOW MANY COINS DID YOU COUNT?

A) 3 **B)** 5 **C)** 8 **D)** 10 **E)** 12

3 WHAT COLOUR WERE THE GEMS IN THE DRAGON'S HEAD?

A) RED **B)** BLUE **C)** GREEN **D)** BLACK **E)** PURPLE

4 HOW MANY SAILS DID THE PIRATE SHIP HAVE?

A) 5 **B)** 4 **C)** 3 **D)** 2 **E)** 1

5 WHAT SYMBOL WAS ON THE MAIN SAIL?

A   B   C   D   E

6 6. WHAT KIND OF SPOOKY CREATURES WERE HAVING A SWORD FIGHT?

A) VAMPIRES **B)** ZOMBIES **C)** SKELETONS **D)** TROLLS **E)** WEREWOLVES

7 7. WHAT COLOUR OF SWORD DIDN'T YOU SEE?

A) RED **B)** BLUE **C)** YELLOW

STUMP SMASH'S
GUIDE TO TROLLS
SEVEN REASONS WHY STUMP SMASH REALLY HATES TROLLS!

1 THEY DESTROYED HIS HOME

Stump Smash was once a magical tree who spent his days slumbering in the warm Skylands sunshine. Then he woke one morning to find out his entire forest had been cut down while he slept. Lumberjack trolls had felled his entire family to fuel their war furnaces.

2 THEY DARED TO PRUNE HIM

Not only had the trolls lopped down his beloved forest, they'd also cut off his branches. He was left with two massive wooden stumps for hands – stumps he soon turned into gigantic hammers to wreak revenge with!

3 THEY SMELL WORSE THAN KAOS

And that's saying something!

4 THEY'RE BIG BULLIES

Trolls join the troll army as soon as they can crawl – sometimes even sooner. They then spend the rest of their lives invading every country on the map. Oh, and building huge, terrifying weapons, of course.

5 THEY'RE ALWAYS TRYING TO BARBEQUE HIS FRIEND, GILL GRUNT!

There are two ways to a troll's heart. One is through a finely crafted battle plan. The other is via its stomach. Trolls will gobble down anything, but are particularly fond of flame-grilled Gillman.

6 THEY WRITE APPALLING POETRY

Usual subjects for troll sonnets include: things that go boom, barbed wire, old rusty nails, large tanks and, most curiously, cucumbers.

7 THEY BLOW UP EVERYTHING THAT MOVES . . . AND QUITE A FEW THINGS THAT DON'T!

Stump enjoys a little nap, but that's impossible with trolls around. The vicious green vandals learn how to lay basic minefields in the nursery and relax by juggling grenades or playing pass-the-plastic explosive. There is one day of the year when all trolls promise not to blow things up, however. On that day, they set fire to stuff instead.

DICE GAME

SOMETIMES, YOUR SKYLANDERS MUST TAKE A CHANCE IN THE FIGHT AGAINST THE DARKNESS. ROLL A DIE AND SEE HOW YOU'D DO IN THESE DANGEROUS SITUATIONS – THE NUMBER IT LANDS ON DECIDES WHAT HAPPENS.

1 PRISM BREAK IS FACING A CYCLOPS MAMMOTH IN THE CENTRE OF MABU MARKET.

 Prism Break zaps the monster with an energy blast. **THE BEAM IS SUPREME.**

The mammoth flattens Prism Break beneath its furry fist. **OUCH!**

He traps it in a shard soul prison. **NO ESCAPE FOR THE CREATURE!**

The beast's foul-smelling fur makes Prism Break faint.

Prism Break's crystalline armour protects him from attack.

 The one-eyed terror butts Prism Break into next week with its ginormous noggin! **WAAH!**

2 DINO-RANG HAS BEEN AMBUSHED BY A BUNCH OF TROLLS IN THE FOREST OF FEAR.

 He takes them all out with a single throw of his stone boomerang. **WALLOP!**

The trolls knock him silly with a lucky shot from their gun snout. **BOOM!**

 They make the mistake of calling him a dragon, so he shows them what an angry dinosaur can do!

A troll greasemonkey whacks Dino-Rang over the head with its wrench. **BACK TO EON'S CASTLE TO RECOVER!**

 He unleashes a flurry of volcanic glass 'rangs. **THE TROLLS DON'T STAND A CHANCE.**

 They tie him up and make him listen to their war poetry. **TORTURE!**

TRIGGER HAPPY JUMPS INTO A PORTAL WITHOUT LOOKING.

He finds himself facing a pack of slavering zombie squirrels. **NUTS!**

He arrives at an all-you-can-shoot shooting gallery. **HEAVEN!**

He tumbles into Kaos's smelly sock drawer **COVER YOUR NOSE, QUICK!**

He discovers a secret stash of gold bullion. **RESULT!**

He squashes Eon's prize pumpkins flat as pancakes. **THE MASTER WON'T BE HAPPY!**

He lands in the tutti frutti ice-cream dunes of the Dessert Desert. **LICK THOSE LIPS.**

 TERRAFIN RECEIVES A SURPRISE BIRTHDAY PRESENT. HE OPENS IT TO DISCOVER THAT IT'S . . .

A sardine and tuna birthday cake! **IT'S FEEDING TIME!**

Another horrible knitted jumper. **ITCHY!**

A shiny new pair of brass knuckles from Bash. **NICE!**

A mini-portal that transports him to Kaos's dungeons! **IT'S A TRAP!**

A year's supply of Shiny Shark toothpaste. **CHOMP CHOMP!**

A free ticket to Gill Grunt's next live concert. **NOOOOOOOOO!**

 SPYRO IS SURROUNDED BY SPOOKS IN A HAUNTED GRAVEYARD.

Spyro gets slimed with sticky ectoplasm. **GROSS!**

He charges at the phantoms, scaring them out of their spectral socks!

The giggling ghosts tie him up with their clanking chains.

Ghost Roaster appears and gobbles up the ghoulies!

Just when he thinks it can't get any worse, zombies burst out of the graves! **HELP!**

His flaming breath sets the spooks' sheets ablaze. **HAUNT THAT!**

Vanishing Voices

SPYRO TOOK A DEEP breath. All eyes were on him as he stood on the platform that had been erected in the shadow of Eon's citadel. A hushed silence fell over the assembled throng as he opened his mouth and roared three words:

"ALL. FIRED. UP!"

The crowd went wild, whooping and clapping. Eruptor was so excited that he accidentally belched a lava pool over Trigger Happy, but Skylands' sharpest shooter didn't mind. That was the most impressive battle cry yet. Surely no one else could do better.

This was the Annual Skylanders Battle Cry Contest. Every year, the Skylanders gathered to see who could shout their battle cries the loudest. Last year, Sonic Boom was crowned champion. She had hollered her battle cry – "FULL SCREAM AHEAD!" – so powerfully that every window in the citadel had smashed at the same time. As had Hugo's glasses!

This year, Hugo was taking no chances. He had wrapped his specs in cotton wool to protect them. The downside was that he couldn't see a thing.

"Well done to Spyro," the little Mabu said as he took to the stage to announce the next contestant. "Argh!" he screamed as he stepped the wrong way and fell off the platform seconds later.

It didn't matter. Sunburn knew he was next in line and swooped down to the podium, fiery feathers blazing bright. He filled his lungs with air and yelled at the top of his voice.

No sound came out. Not even a squeak. Sunburn tried again. Still nothing. He was completely mute.

In the crowd, Trigger Happy turned to ask Eruptor what was happening, but found that he had no voice either. In fact, Eruptor was the same, as was Spyro. What had happened? It was as if something, or someone, had stolen their voices.

That someone was hiding in the bushes watching the Skylanders' confusion. Giggling to himself, Kaos popped a cork into the neck of a dusty old bottle.

"Did the spell work?" Glumshanks asked, peering through the leaves.

"Did it work?" Kaos hissed. "DID IT WORK? My brilliant spell has stolen the Skyblunderers' stupid, shouty voices."

"Trapping them inside that bottle."

"Inside the Mysterious and Ancient Decanter of Hush-Hush, yes." Kaos held up the bottle so Glumshanks could see the tiny lights dancing behind the glass, one for each of the Skylanders. "They are doomed to be silent for ever. DOOMED I tell you!"

"There's no need to shout," Glumshanks thought, although he would never dream of saying such a thing out loud. He decided to focus on the plan instead. "So, while the Skylanders are wondering what happened to their vocal chords, we slip into the Core of Light and throw a spanner in the works, right?"

"Not a spanner," Kaos cackled. "Something far more devastating."

With a flourish, he produced a foul-smelling sock from his sleeve, nearly gassing Glumshanks with its repellent reek. "My old sock will bung up the mechanism, the Core of Light will grind to a halt and the Darkness will conquer Skylands!"

On the stage, Sunburn looked out over the crowd in despair. Everyone was shouting at each other – or trying to, at least. Then he smelled something. Something eye-wateringly bad. Where was it coming from? He sniffed and followed his nose, spotting two tiny figures sneaking towards the Core of Light. Kaos and Glumshanks! They must be behind this.
Sunburn tried to get his fellow Skylanders' attention, but couldn't make a sound. It was useless.
There was only one thing for it. Flapping his wings, Sunburn shot into the air, his feathers immediately bursting into flames.

Spyro glanced up. Was something on fire? His eyes widened as he saw Sunburn. The dragon was streaking across the sky, leaving a trail of fire in his wake. A trail of fire that was forming words!
"LOOK OUT", Spyro read, "IT'S KAOS!"
The sizzling Sunburn then dropped into a daring dive, drawing a flaming arrow towards . . . Kaos himself!

"ARRRGH!" Kaos shrieked as the Skylanders charged angrily towards him and his hapless accomplice. "Time to leave, Glumshanks!"

The evil Portal Master spun around, only to have his path blocked as Sunburn landed in front of him. He flung his arms into the air in shock, sending both the Mysterious and Ancient Decanter of Hush Hush and his stinking sock into the air – and what goes up, must come down. The sock slapped onto Glumshanks' face, and the bottle smashed into a thousand pieces on the floor.

The stolen voices swarmed into the air before zooming back to their rightful owners. Sunburn swallowed hard as one of the bright lights flew straight into his mouth.

"Woah, what was that?" he said and his eyes widened.

His voice was back! A smile spread across his beak.

"ROAST 'N' TOAST!" he yelled, bellowing his battle cry right into Kaos' face. The defeated Portal Master yelped, then snapped his fingers. There was a flash of light and he disappeared, dragging the gagging Glumshanks with him.

"Great work, Sunburn!" cried Spyro. "That was the loudest battle cry yet."

"Indeed it was," puffed Hugo, as he ran towards them clutching the trophy. "I hereby declare Sunburn this year's champion."

Every Skylander in the crowd cheered at the same time. In fact, the noise was so deafening that Hugo's glasses instantly smashed.

"Not again," he whimpered quietly.

The End

GURGLEFIN'S FIN-TICKLERS!

NOW THAT LUCKY LAGOON IS BACK TO NORMAL, GURGLEFIN HAS RETURNED TO HIS GOOD-NATURED SELF . . . WHICH UNFORTUNATELY MEANS IT'S BAD JOKE TIME. HE JUST LOVES SHARING HIS HORRENDOUS HOWLERS. RATE EACH OF HIS GAGS BY SHADING IN THE LAUGH-O-METER.

What happened to the shark who swallowed a bunch of keys?
HE GOT LOCK JAW!

Where do you find out how heavy a whale is?
AT A WHALE WEIGH STATION!

Where do salmon wash?
IN A RIVER BASIN!

Why did the octopus cross the road?
TO GET TO THE OTHER TIDE!

What do you get from a bad-tempered shark?
AS FAR AWAY AS POSSIBLE!

What fish goes zooming along at 100mph?
A MOTOR PIKE!

What do you call a fish with no eyes?
FSH!

What kind of fish helps you hear better?
A HERRING AID!

Why are goldfish orange?
THE WATER MAKES THEM RUSTY!

What do sea monsters eat?
FISH AND SHIPS!

Knock Knock.
Who's there?
FISH!
Fish who?
BLESS YOU!

TONGUE-TWISTER!
Try saying this quickly three times:

A NOISY NOISE ANNOYS AN OYSTER!

54

MASTER EON
EXCLUSIVE INTERVIEW!

EON, THE GREATEST PORTAL MASTER OF THEM ALL, TALKS TO HUGO ABOUT LIFE, BUSHY BEARDS AND GIANT TOMATOES . . .

Hugo: Thank you for taking time out of your busy schedule to talk to us, Master Eon.

Eon: My pleasure. Anything to help those brand new Portal Masters out there.

Hugo: Did you always want to be a Portal Master?

Eon: You don't decide to become a Portal Master. The universe decides for you. In my case it all started when I was a humble servant boy for the great Portal Master Nattybumpo.

H: What was Nattybumpo like?

E: He was a very wise man. And a very large man too. Liked his pies, did Nattybumpo. He also had the biggest, bushiest, reddest beard you've ever seen. It was so big, birds used to nest in it in spring. He was always pulling twigs out of it over breakfast.

H: Did he train you in the ways of Portal Mastery?

E: Not at first. I just polished the pans in his kitchens. As he loved his pies there were always a lot of pans. I worked hard and one day, when I was about eight, was asked if I would polish his Portal of Power. It was such an honour.

H: What happened?

E: Well, the moment I took my duster to it, the Portal activated and transported Nattybumpo into the middle of the dirt seas. I don't know who was more suprised, him or me. He was only wearing a pair of pants and his fluffy slippers. It must have been a bit of a shock for the dirt sharks sunbathing on the dunes.

H: Was he angry?

E: Not old Nattybumpo. He saw the funny side of it - although he did get quite a lot of sand in his Y-fronts. I transported him back and he began my training. I've never looked back.

H. What is the most important lesson for a trainee Portal Master?

E. Look before you leap. You don't want to transport yourself - or your Skylanders - into danger. Oh, and make sure you're fully dressed before you let anyone touch your portal. Just in case.

H: What do you think you'd do if you weren't a Portal Master?

E: I would grow prize vegetables. You know, really big ones. Tomatoes the size of sheep - that kind of thing.

H: Please don't mention sheep.

E: I've told you before that you've nothing to fear from sheep . . .

H: I'm not so sure . . .

E: Except the big, angry-looking one standing right behind you with a massive sword of course!

H: What?
ARRRGGGHH!!!!!

E: Ha ha ha ha! Just kidding. I love that joke. Never gets tired.

H: Hmph. Very funny.

WHO-DUNNIT?

IT'S TIME TO TURN DETECTIVE. SOMEONE HAS (ACCIDENTALLY, WE'RE SURE) LET A FLOCK OF SHEEP INTO HUGO'S LIBRARY. ANSWER THE QUESTIONS TO FIND OUT THE CULPRIT FROM THE TEN SKYLANDER SUSPECTS.

**THERE ARE TEN SUSPECTS.
EXAMINE THE CLUES BELOW IN ORDER.
EACH WILL HELP YOU ELIMINATE ONE OF THE SKYLANDERS. WHEN YOU'RE CONVINCED THEY DIDN'T DO IT, CROSS OUT THEIR BOX.
THE ONE WHO'S LEFT IS THE CULPRIT.**

CLUE 1

The guilty suspect does not have wings. Cross out anyone who does!

CLUE 2

Witnesses say the culprit does not have green eyes. Does that help?

CLUE 3

There was no lingering smell of burning left in the library, so no Fire elementals were involved. Cross them out!

CLUE 4

On the day it happened, Slam Bam was attending an ice sculpture competition on the other side of Skylands – so he couldn't have done it.

CLUE 5

Footprints on the floor show that the guilty party walks on two legs. Cross out anyone who doesn't!

CLUE 6

Some red hairs were found among the sheep, so the perpetrator must have red hair!

SO, WHO LET THE SHEEP INTO THE LIBRARY?
HAVE YOU ELIMINATED EVERY INNOCENT PARTY FROM YOUR INVESTIGATION? IS THERE ONLY ONE SUSPECT LEFT? TURN TO PAGE 62 TO FIND OUT IF YOU'VE POINTED THE FINGER OF GUILT AT THE RIGHT SKYLANDER!

STORM OF SKULLS

HEX HAS UNLEASHED A STORM OF SKULLS. CAN YOU FIND THE SEVEN SKULLS THAT ARE SLIGHTLY DIFFERENT FROM THE REST?

DID YOU KNOW?

Many inhabitants of Skylands are wary of Hex and suspect that she has used her potent magical abilities for evil. Eon and her fellow Skylanders know differently – she is an ally to be trusted!

A DAY IN THE LIFE OF...

Lightning Rod!

7-8AM:
Breakfast. Had the usual 400 eggs on toast. Morning papers were full of my exploits. Apparently I've saved the Cloud Kingdom 827 times this year so far. Well, everyone needs a hobby.

9AM-1PM:
The Storm Giant Games are almost upon us. Spent morning practising for the Thousand-Metre Lightning Bolt Hurl. Kept overshooting and managed to electrocute Eruptor three times. Whoops!

1PM-2PM:
Had a light lunch at Charlie's Celestial Cafe. Ate fifteen cows, eight boar and two horses. Still a bit peckish. Might have a small llama to keep my strength up.

2PM-3PM:
Popped to the shops to pick up a new cloud. The old one keeps shrinking in the wash. Noticed they've built a new statue of me in the town square. Don't think they've got my nose right. Fixed it with a little bolt from the blue.

3PM-4PM:
Afternoon training interrupted by Kaos. The little wimp was trying to destroy Skylands. Again. Sent him packing, but let the other Skylanders help a bit. I can't always take all the glory.

4PM-5PM:
Read through fan mail. Today's mailbag was so big it took fourteen postmen to deliver it.

5PM-7PM:
Quick spot of training before tea. Bumped into the other Games contestants down at the Storm Giant Stadium. They really are girlie, you know. Especially the girls.

7PM-8PM:
Tea time. Didn't fancy much so only had three sheep.

8PM-11PM:
Curled up in my cloud to relax with my favourite book – "Rod the Bod" by, well, me. It's ever so good.

11PM:
Time for my beauty sleep. Ha! That's a good one. As if I need it!

THE FINAL TEST!

WELL, YOUNG PORTAL MASTER, YOU'VE ALMOST REACHED THE END OF YOUR TRAINING. IT'S TIME TO FIND OUT HOW MUCH YOU HAVE LEARNED. TAKE OUR TITANIC TEST TO SEE IF YOU REALLY MAKE THE GRADE! YOU'LL FIND THE ANSWERS OVER THE PAGE. GOOD LUCK!

1. WHAT IS THE SOURCE OF ALL EVIL?
a) The Gloominess b) The Darkness
c) The Ooh-it's-a-bit-murky-ness

2. WHAT IS THE NAME OF KAOS' BUTLER?
a) Glumshanks b) Miserableshanks
c) Forelornshanks

3. HOW MANY ELEMENTS MAKE UP THE CORE OF LIGHT?
a) Seven b) Eight c) Nine

4. WHAT IS THE SKYLANDERS' FAVOURITE HOLIDAY DESTINATION?
a) Blistering Beach b) Dessert Desert
c) Royal City of Arkus

5. WHAT KIND OF CREATURE IS SANDYFUZZ?
a) Drow b) Molekin c) Mabu

7. WHO KIDNAPPED GILL GRUNT'S MERMAID GIRLFRIEND?
a) Trolls b) Pirates c) Sheep

8. WHAT WAS THE NAME OF THE BAKER THAT PERSUADED THE UNDEAD TO EAT PIES INSTEAD OF PEOPLE?
a) Pummelson b) Clobberson
c) Batterson

9. WHO IS THIS?
a) Flynn
b) Cali
c) Hugo

6. WHICH DRAGON IS HALF PLANT?

a) Spyro   b) Whirlwind   c) Camo

10 WHAT WAS THE CAPITAL CITY OF THE ARKEYAN EMPIRE CALLED?
a) Royal City of Archon **b)** Royal City of Archie **c)** Royal City of Arkus

11. WHICH OF THESE SKYLANDERS WASN'T CREATED BY THE ARKEYANS?

a) Drill Sergeant
b) Drobot
c) Chop Chop

12 WHAT IS THIS?
a) Rocket Imp
b) Flame Imp
c) Earth Imp

13 WHERE IS THE LUCKIEST PLACE IN SKYLANDS?
a) Fortune Forest **b)** Serendip City
c) Lucky Lagoon

14 WHY DID GURGLEFIN FALL OVER?
a) He tripped on a beetle **b)** He was wearing a new pair of roller skates
c) The ground was covered in ice

15 WHAT DOES 'AHOY' MEAN TO PIRATES?
a) Hello **b)** Goodbye **c)** Go away

16 WHAT IS THE NAME OF THE MOST VILLAINOUS PIRATE EVER TO SAIL THE 7024 SEAS?
a) Captain Fearbeard **b)** Captain Dreadbeard **c)** Captain Anxietybeard

17 THERE IS ONE DAY OF THE YEAR WHEN TROLLS PROMISE NOT TO DO WHAT?
a) Blow stuff up **b)** Hug a sheep
c) Knit a jumper

18 WHO WAS LAST YEAR'S SKYLANDERS BATTLE CRY CHAMPION?
a) Camo **b)** Sonic Boom
c) Wrecking Ball

19 WHY COULDN'T THE SKYLANDERS USE THEIR VOICES?
a) They all had colds **b)** Kaos stole them **c)** They'd promised not to talk

20 EON WAS AN APPRENTICE TO WHICH PORTAL MASTER?
a) Smartypantso **b)** Tidyboilo
c) Nattybumpo

HOW DID YOU DO?

0-4 answers correct
Hmmmm. Have you been paying attention? I suggest you start back at the beginning of the annual.

5-15 answers correct
Well done! You have learned well. You are on the way to becoming a great Portal Master!

16-20 answers correct
Absolutely brilliant. You are a Portal Master to rival Master Eon himself.

ANSWERS

PAGE 24-25 SKYLANDER SEARCH
1. CAMO
2. CHOP CHOP
3. CYNDER
4. DOUBLE TROUBLE
5. DRILL SERGEANT
6. DROBOT
7. ERUPTOR
8. FLAMESLINGER
9. GHOST ROASTER
10. GILL GRUNT
11. HEX
12. LIGHTNING ROD
13. PRISM BREAK
14. SLAM BAM
15. SONIC BOOM
16. SPYRO
17. STEALTH ELF
18. STUMP SMASH
19. TRIGGER HAPPY
20. WARNADO
21. WHAM SHELL
22. WHIRLWIND
23. WRECKING BALL
24. ZAP
25. ZOOK

The hidden agent of Kaos is a Spell Punk

PAGE 27 SHADOW FIGHT
Shadow 3.

PAGE 28 SKYLANDS SUPERBRAIN
Across
1. Lockmaster Imp
5. Zeppelin
7. Portal Master
10. Darkness
11. Kaos
13. Hugo
14. Glumshanks
18. Core of Light
20. Tree of Life

Down
2. Arkeyans
3. Spell Punks
4. Elements
6. Persephone
8. Trolls
9. Cali
12. Eon
15. Portals
16. Sheep
17. Cyclops
19. Flynn

PAGE 36 SPOT THE DIFFERENCE
The square that is exactly the same is 3C.

PAGE 38-39 - WHEELSPIN!

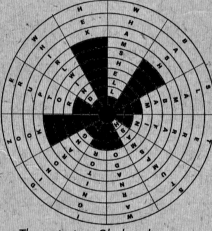

The missing Skylander is Prism Break

PAGE 42 MESSAGE IN A BOTTLE!
The message reads:
Dreadbeard's mum used to call him fluffy! How sweet!

PAGE 43 CRUSTY CODEBREAKER
The secret message reads: Kaos is short, bald and incredibly smelly. He wants to take over Skylands.

PAGE 44 SAY WHAT?
SPYRO
"ALL FIRED UP!"

TRIGGER HAPPY
"NO GOLD, NO GLORY!"

STEALTH ELF
"SILENT BUT DEADLY!"

BASH
"ROCK AND ROLL!"

PRISM BREAK
"THE BEAM IS SUPREME!"

SONIC BOOM
"FULL SCREAM AHEAD!"

DOUBLE TROUBLE
"BOOM SHOCK-A-LA!"

GILL GRUNT
"FEAR THE FISH"

PAGE 46 OBSERVATION DECK
1. A
2. D
3. B
4. D
5. C
6. C
7. A

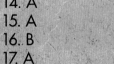

PAGE 56 WHO-DUNNIT?
The Skylander who let the sheep into the library was Trigger Happy!

PAGE 60-61 THE FINAL TEST
1. B
2. A
3. B
4. A
5. C
6. C
7. B
8. C
9. A
10. C
11. B
12. A
13. C
14. A
15. A
16. B
17. A
18. B
19. B
20. C